BLACK HUMOUR

Adam Smith

For information contact : book_author@yahoo.com

Book and Cover design by Versoo

ISBN-13: 978-1544189550
ISBN-10: 1544189559

First Edition: February 2017

2 1

What is black humour?

"Black humour is humour that deals with unpleasant aspects of life in a bitter or ironic way"

"Black humour is when, for example, a man takes off his belt to hang himself, and his trousers fall down. Another example of black humour, "Suicide just isn't funny, no matter which way you slice it," is an effective satire at the way that suicide is treated in mainstream western culture, insinuating that attitudes towards suicide are even more morose or morbid than the act or mental condition leading to it."

"A new study in the journal Cognitive Processing has found that intelligence plays a key role in the appreciation of black humour – as well as several other factors, notably a person's aggression levels."

Attention: This book contain comedy, satire, jokes, etc., that presents tragic, distressing, or morbid situations in humorous terms; humour that is ironic, cynical, or dry;

Warning: contain adult or sexual content and is meant for mature audience

-1-

What's the difference between a Taliban outpost and a Pakistani elementary school?
I don't know, I just fly the drone!

-2-

A guy was walking to a bar and on his way he found a girl tied up to the railroad tracks. He untied her and they had sex. Guy gets to the bar, friends ask why he's so late, tells them about the girl he found and all the different positions they fucked in.
Friends give him props and ask if he got head, guy replies "I couldn't find it."

-3-

A man goes into a library and asks the librarian for a book on suicide.
The librarian says: "fuck off you won't bring it back".

-4-

A guy goes into the library and asks the librarian "do you have the new book on small penises?"
She replies "sorry, I don't think it's in yet."
He says, "yeah, that's the one."

-5-

What's the difference between John Wayne and Jack Daniels?
Jack Daniels is still killing Indians!

-6-

What's the difference between Hitler and Michael Phelps?
Michael Phelps can finish a race.

-7-

Why is aspirin white?
Because it works!

-8-

Why don't black people use aspirin?
Because they don't like picking the piece of cotton off the top.

-9-

How many cops does it take to change a lightbulb?
Two; one to beat the room for being black and one to arrest the lightbulb for being broke.

-10-

US and Ethiopia national teams played a friendly the other day.
The final score was USA 8-Ethiopia didn't.

-11-

The term "Every 60 seconds in Africa..." is really stupid.
Everyone knows Africans don't get seconds. They're lucky if they get a single serving.

-12-

What makes an ISIS joke funny?
The execution!

-13-

My best friend got mad at me because he caught me sniffing his sisters panties. It didn't help that they were still on her. Or that all of his family was there too. It really made the rest of her funeral really awkward.

-14-

How do you start a rave in Ethiopia?
Nail a piece of toast to the ceiling.

-15-

Have you ever had Ethiopian food? No?

Neither have they!

-16-

Why if Princess Diana like Pink Floyd?
Her last big hit was The Wall!

-17-

Why does Hellen Keller wear tight pants?
So, you can read her lips!

-18-

Why does Hellen Keller masturbate using only one hand?
So she can moan with the other.

-19-

How did Hellen Keller's parents punish her?
They rearranged the furniture.

-20-

A sadist, necrophiliac, pyromaniac, zoophiliac, and a masochist were sitting in a jail cell together.
The zoophiliac says, "I want to have sex with a cat."
The sadist says, "I want to torture a cat then have sex with it."
The pyromaniac says, "I wanna torture the cat, set it on fire, then have sex with it."
The necrophiliac says, "Well I want to torture the cat,

set it on fire, have sex with it, then kill it and have sex with it again."

Finally, the masochist says, "Meow."

-21-

How many potatoes does it take to kill an Irish man?

None!

-22-

A woman brings eight-year-old Johnny home and tells his mother that he was caught playing doctors and nurses with Mary, her eight-year-old daughter. Johnny's mother says, "Let's not be too harsh on them... they are bound to be curious about sex at that age."

"Curious about sex?" replies Mary's mother. "He's taken her fucking appendix out!"

-23-

How many cats does it take to paint a wall?

Depends on how hard you throw them!

-24-

A man walks into his bedroom holding a Duck.

His wife asks: "why are you holding that Duck?"

The man: "this is the pig I'd like to fuck."

The wife: "that's not a pig, that's a Duck."

The man: "I was talking to the Duck."

-25-

What's Al Qaeda's favorite football team?
The New York Jets!

-26-

What's Osama Bin Laden's favourite drink?
A double Manhattan.

-27-

How do you turn a fruit into a vegetable?
Aids.

-28-

So my wife walked in on me fucking my son, I don't know what is more shocking, the look on my wife's face or the fact that the abortion clinic let me keep him.

-29-

A father is showering in the morning when his young daughter stumbles into the bathroom.
She opens the curtain and notices his penis to which she says, "Daddy what's that?"
Seeing it as a teachable moment the father replies, "That's my penis sweetie."
The daughter quickly asks, "Will I ever get one?"
The father chuckles and responds, "As soon as your mother leaves for work."

-30-

What's the worst part about being a black Jew?
You have to sit in the back of the oven.

-31-

Why does Eric Clapton use a Mac?
Because windows killed his son!

-32-

What's the hardest thing about microwaving a vegetable?
Fitting the wheelchair through the door!

-33-

Why can't Stevie Wonder drive a bus?
There is no steering wheel at the back of the bus!

-34-

"**Y**our generation is too reliant on technology," said my grandpa.
"No, your generation is too reliant on technology," I retorted as I pulled the plug on his life support to further prove my point.

-35-

What's red and crawls up your leg?
A homesick miscarriage!

-36-

What did the hotdog vendor say when he was pulled from the WTC rubble?
So who ordered the two jumbos?

-37-

So, I was walking around town yesterday and passed by a gun store. Intrigued, I entered to find that everything was half off.
I didn't know that Back to School sales had already started.

-38-

A man called 911 and said "Come quick, my son swallowed a condom!"
5 minutes later, he called again and said, "never mind, I found another one".

-39-

Statistically, 9 out of 10 people enjoy gang rape!

-40-

What's Belgium famous for?
Chocolates and child abuse, and they only invented the chocolates to get to the kids.

-41-

How do you neuter a tasmanian?
Kick his sister in the jaw.

So, a girl goes to her dad and asks if she can borrow the car.

He tells her: "You know what you need to do."

So, she gets on her knees pulls his cock out and starts sucking it.

After a bit she pops it out of her mouth looks up at him and says: "Gee dad, your dick tastes like shit."

He slaps his forehead and says: "Oh that's right. Your brother has the car."

What breaks when you give it to a two year old?
Their pelvis!

What's round and hates Pakis?
The world!

What's worse than the Holocaust?
Six million Jews.

What's 16" long, stiff and makes women scream?
Cot death!

A man is driving along a narrow mountain road, and as he approaches a turn he can see a plume of smoke rising from the mountain side. As he turns the corner he sees that a car has come off the road and crashed into the valley below. A little girl has been thrown out of the car before it fell, and is standing beside the side of the road looking down.

He pulls over and walks over to the little girl. Below, he can see the car is on fire, and there are people trapped inside, hammering on the windows trying to get out.

The man asks: "Is that your family down there?"

She tearfully nods in reply.

He turns to her and says: "Boy, you are just having the worst day aren't you?" as he undoes his fly.

-48-

A man and a boy are walking in a forest at night.

The boy says: "Sure is creepy out here."

The man says: "You're telling me! I have to walk out of here alone."

-49-

What do you call an Ethiopian with a dog?

A vegetarian.

-50-

What is black and sits at the top of the stairs smoking?

Stephen Hawking after a house fire.

-51-

What do you tell a woman with two black eyes?
Nothing, you told her twice.

-52-

What is Osama bin Laden favorite chocolate bar?
Double Decker!

-53-

What's the difference between a bag of cocaine and Eric Clapton's son?
Eric wouldn't let a bag of cocaine fall out the balcony window.

-54-

What is pink and wrinkly and hangs out your PJ's?
Your mum.

-55-

People are so politically correct these days you can't even say black paint.
Instead you have to say: "Leroy, please paint my fence".

-56-

Asians drive so bad that I'm starting to think that Pearl Harbor was an accident.

-57-

What's worse than spilled milk?
The Holocaust.

-58-

What would George Washington be doing if he were alive right now?
Screaming and scratching at the top of his coffin.

-59-

What's the difference between Elliot Rodger and an egg?
An egg gets laid before it cracks.

-60-

A girl goes out to a bar and meets a nice African American gentleman. They hit it off, and end up going back to her place for some extra.
They're kissing and groping, the girl unbuttons the man's pants, and the asks the man, "Before we go any further, I need to know. Is the stereotype true?"
The black man looks at her and says, "Of course it is."
He then stabbed her and ran off with her purse.

-61-

A priest, a pedophile, and a rapist walk into a bar.
And that's just the first guy.

-62-

A beautiful woman was standing on the edge of a bridge, about to jump off. An old stinky bum walks

up and she sees him approaching.
She says: "Go away! There's nothing you can say that'll stop me!"
"Well if you're going to kill yourself anyway, why not have sex with me? At least I'll enjoy it."
"No! That's disgusting!", she says, and the old bum shrugs and starts walking away.
"Wait!", she says. "Is that all you're going to say?! Where are you going?!"
"Down to the bottom. If I hurry, you'll still be warm."

-63-

What's the difference between a grade school and an Terrorist training camp?
Look... I just fly the drone.

-64-

Two guys in a communal shower:
Guy1: You want to play the rape game?
Guy2: No.
Guy1: That's the spirit!

-65-

Why does NASA drink Sprite?
Because they couldn't get 7up.

-66-

Why don't cannibals eat clowns?
Because they taste funny.

-67-

Dentist: "This will hurt a little."
Patient: "OK."
Dentist: "I've been having an affair with your wife for a while now."

-68-

I was hiking once with my girlfriend. Suddenly a huge brown bear was charging at us, really mad. We must have come close to her cubs.

Luckily I had my 9mm pistol with me. One shot to my girlfriend's kneecap was all it took. I could walk away at a comfortable pace.

-69-

*E*ven people who are good for nothing have the capacity to bring a smile to your face, for instance when you push them down the stairs.

-70-

A priests asks the convicted murderer at the electric chair, "Do you have any last requests?"
"Yes," replies the murderer. "Can you please hold my hand?"

-71-

-*M*om, I'm still having those sharp headaches!
-Well why don't you move away from in front of the

dart board then?!

-72-

Let's eat mom.
Let's eat, mom.
Punctuation. It can save lives!

-73-

Patient: Oh doctor, I'm just so nervous. This is my first operation.
Doctor: Don't worry. Mine too.

-74-

"**Y**ou da bomb!"
"No, you da bomb!"
In America – a compliment. In the Middle East – an argument.

-75-

Doctor: You're obese.
Patient: Whoa, for that I definitely want a second opinion.
Doctor: You're quite ugly, too.

-76-

I saw two kids fighting in the elementary school playground. Being the only adult around, I had to step in. They didn't stand a chance.

16

-77-

- **W**ow, honey, I never thought our son would go that far!

-Yeah, the catapult is really amazing. Go get our daughter!

-78-

Tombstone engraving: *I TOLD you I was sick!*

-79-

At a first date:

He: "I work with animals every day!"
She: "Oh how sweet! What is it that you do?"
He: "I'm a butcher."

-80-

Q: Have you heard they found a dead guy with his head buried in his cornflakes?
A: The police believed it was a cereal killer.

-81-

A stressed-looking mom and little Johnny run around the beach.

After about fifteen minutes the mom stops, out of breath and demands: „Come on Johnny, please remember where you buried daddy in the sand, will you?".

-82-

An artist asked the gallery manager if anybody asked about his paintings.

"Well, there's good news and there's bad news," said the owner.

"The good one is that a gentleman liked your work and asked if its value would appreciate after your death. When I said yes, he bought all 20 of your paintings."

"But that's fantastic," whooped the artist. "What could possibly be the bad news?"

"The gentleman was your doctor."

-83-

This morning I saw what will probably become the worst air disaster in the Midwest. An ultralight single-seater plane crashed into a cemetery in Stockholm, Wisconsin.

So far, the search and rescue teams have recovered 1736 bodies and as the digging continues into the night, we can only expect that number to climb.

-84-

A blind man with a guide dog comes to a town square, takes the dog by the tail and starts whirling him around.

„What on earth are you doing?!", asks a passer-by.

The blind man replies, „Nothing, just looking around a bit."

-85-

Doctor: "You look much worse than you did last week! I said you should smoke a maximum of five cigarettes a day!"
Patient: "And that's what I did. And it wasn't easy because up until now I didn't smoke at all!".

-86-

What is yellow and makes moms happy in the morning?
The school bus.

-87-

One cannibal complains to another, "Man I'm having a terrible constipation lately!"
-"See? I told you not to eat so many government clerks!"

-88-

Dentist's tombstone: Here lies Frank Serra, filling his last cavity.

-89-

Do you think there's no good news about having Alzheimer's?
You can buy and wrap your own surprise presents. Plus you are constantly making new friends.

-90-

A guy asked at a skydiving school, "If the chute

doesn't open and the reserve doesn't open either, how long until we hit the ground?"
The instructor looked at him and said, "The rest of your life."

-91-

But mum, I don't want to go to America.
- Hush child and keep swimming.

-92-

Q: Why did the one-armed man cross the road?
A: To get to the second hand shop.

-93-

Why have trips to England become so popular with Siamese twins?
It gives the other one a chance to drive a car, too.

-94-

Two Arabs sit in the Gaza Strip, enjoying a quiet pint of goat milk.
One takes out his wallet and starts flipping through the pictures.
-This is my oldest son. He's a martyr. This here is my second son. He's also a martyr!
-The second Arab nods, "They blow up so fast, don't they?"

-95-

Two cannibals are chewing a clown.
One says to the other: "Hey, does it taste kinda funny to you?"

-96-

A man visits a doctor for a checkup. When it's over, the doctor tells him he has bad news.
"You have only six months to live."
The man digests it for a while and then says, "There's just one thing I can do, I have to become a Communist."
Surprised, the doctor asks, "But you've been a patriotic American all your life, why would you become a Communist now?"
The man says, "Better when one of them dies than one of us!"

-97-

I broke up with my Japanese girlfriend today.
I had to drop the bomb two or three times before she finally got it.

-98-

Man is asked at the hospital:
-How tall are you?
-5'8'', doctor.
-I'm very sorry, but I'm not the doctor. I'm the carpenter.

-99-

21

Two turkeys are looking at the sky at dusk and one asks the other: „Do you believe in life after Christmas?"

-100-

Doctor: Your test results are showing you'll easily live to be 80.
Patient: But, wait, I am 80 just now.
Doctor: See, I told you to live healthier!

-101-

A doctor tells a patient, "Sir, you are highly contagious and must be placed in isolation. Until we get in contact with the CDC (Centers for Disease Control and Prevention), your diet will consist of pizza and fried eggs."
"Will that help me get better again?" asks the patient.
"Not really. But it's the only thing we can shove in under the door."

-102-

Black humor is like a pair of healthy kidneys.
Not everyone has it.

-103-

A doctor walks in a cemetery one afternoon when a hand shoots through the earth and grabs his ankle.
A hollow voice speaks from underneath the ground, "You're a doctor, right? Do you have anything against

worms?"

-104-

A guy had to move abroad and had to sell his dog.
The new owner asks, "And does he like little kids?"
"Sure, but it's cheaper to just buy him dog biscuits."

-105-

Black humor is a lot like food really. Not everyone
gets it.

-106-

They say you cannot outrun a bear.
*True, but don't panic, usually it is enough to outrun
the chubbiest member of your hiking group.*

-107-

Two cannibals are enjoying dinner.
One compliments the other, "I say, Bill, your wife
really makes a great meal."

-108-

Around 50% of our youth sees the future in a positive
way.
*The other half doesn't have the money to buy the
drugs.*

-109-

How did the dentist suddenly become a brain

surgeon?
A slip of the hand.

-110-

What is black and sticks to a tree?
A peeping tom after a forest fire.

-111-

Never break someone's heart, they only have one.
Break their bones instead, they have 206 of them.

-112-

"**M**other I really don't like the red soup"
"Be quiet child. We get it just once a month"

-113-

If I ever need a heart transplant, I'd want the heart of my ex-wife.
She's never used it.

-114-

A mom tells her son a joke; the son is embarrassed and says: "Mom, please don't tell any more jokes. You really can't make them."
The mom only shrugs and says, "Well – I did make you..."

-115-

Either the woman at the back of the train has two really ugly children, or two seriously cool Pokémons.

-116-

For Sale: Parachute. Used once, never opened, small stain.

-117-

Doctor tells his patient, "I'm afraid you are going to die in a few hours. What is your last wish?"
-Patient replies, "I need a good doctor."

-118-

How to save a man from drowning?
Try removing your foot from their head.

-119-

What do you get when you cross a rabbit and a pit bull?
Just the pit bull.

-120-

"Mother, why do people die so quickly in our family?"
...
"Mama?"
"Mama?"
"Maaaammaaaaaaa!"

-121-

What do you call people who use the temperature method of contraception?
Parents.

-122-

Why do hurricanes get such lame names, like Sandy? Name that thing Hurricane Death Megatron 696 and I guarantee folks will be evacuating like they need to.

-123-

A magician comes to a seniors' home for entertainment afternoon: "Aaaaand? Is everybody heeere?"
Seniors, enthusiastically, "Yeaaaah!"
Magician, winking, "But not for looooong... !"

-124-

- Mommy, mommy, I found daddy!
- How often do I have to tell you not to dig around in the garden!

-125-

Remember that moment when you notice that one fork isn't really very clean when you're laying the table and you have to decide which family member you like the least.

-127-

Famous last words of a bomb disposal expert?
"Yes, the red wire."

-128-

What did the cannibal do once he dumped his lady friend?
He wiped his bottom.

-129-

A dyslexic man walks into a bra...

-130-

When a blind woman tells her boyfriend that she is seeing someone, it could either be a really terrible news or a really great news.

-131-

If you see me smiling, I'm probably thinking of doing something evil.
If I'm laughing, I've already done it.

-132-

Strong people don't put other people down.
They lift them up and slam them to the ground for maximum impact.

-133-

-Doctor, please, my son ate some cement. What can I do?
-First of all, don't give him anything to drink…

-134-

Join the Army, meet some fascinating people, then kill them.

-135-

A chubbier woman: Mirror, Mirror on the wall, who's the fairest of them all?
Mirror: "Kindly move aside. I can't see anything."

-136-

Doctor: And how is it going with your old ailment, Mr. Smith?
Patient: Very well, I've been divorced for half a year now.

-137-

A lady tells the nurse at a maternity hospital, "I want to call my little baby Ellie."
Nurse replies, "I'm sorry, but that name is already taken, perhaps you can consider naming her Ellie532 or Ellie_153?".

-138-

If you need to break up with somebody, the best place to do so is McDonalds.

There are no plates or glasses to be broken over your head, no sharp knives or spiky forks, plus you can always hide behind a fat kid.

-139-

Patient: Doctor, I'm starting to forget things.
Doctor: I understand.
Patient: Understand what?

-140-

Give a man a match, and he'll be warm for a few hours.
Set him on fire, and he will be warm for the rest of his life.

-141-

There is nothing more depressing than a failed suicide attempt.

-142-

What is brown, small, and smells of caramel?
A diabetic who's been struck by lightning.

-143-

I visited my new friend in his flat.
He told me to make myself at home.
So, I threw him out. I hate having visitors.

-144-

My Chinese friend got really sick one day and had to go to a hospital.

I went to see him the next day, but he just kept whispering "Chun Yu Yan" over and over – and then died.

I was very sad and googled his last message after the burial.

Apparently, it means "You're standing on my oxygen tube."

-145-

They say the surest way to a man's heart is through the stomach.

But personally, I find going through the ribcage a lot easier.

-146-

I took my wife's family out for biscuits and tea.

They weren't very happy about having to donate blood though.

-147-

Cremation. My final hope for a smokin' hot body!

-148-

"**I**'m on a hunt for my wife's murderer, have been for years."

"Oh my God! Your wife's been murdered?!"

"No, no, you misunderstand. I'm still looking for

him."

-149-

My Grandfather has the heart of a lion and a lifetime ban from the Atlanta Zoo.

-150-

Son: "Mommy, mommy, daddy hanged himself in the attic!"
Mother: "What??!!"
Son: "Gotcha, April's fool! He hangs in the garage."

-151-

I was digging in our garden and found a chest full of gold coins. I wanted to run straight home to tell my wife about it.
Then I remembered why I'm digging in our garden.

-152-

A man who wants to murder his wife goes in a pharmacy and asks for cyanide.
"I'm sorry sir, but I can't give you cyanide just like that."
Without a word, the man takes out his wife's photograph and holds it in front of him.
The pharmacist apologizes, "My mistake, I didn't realize you had a prescription."

-153-

I want a divorce!

-But you made a vow in the church that we remain together till death do us part.

-I guess you are right. Very well, go ahead and drink up the tea I made for you.

-154-

*W*hat do Ironman and Sarah Palin have in common?
They both had a Downey Jr. inside them!

-155-

A black third grader goes to his mom and says:"
Mom , I have the biggest dick in the third grade. Is that because I'm black?"
Mom replies: "No, it's because you're 19".

-156-

*W*hat's black underneath and white on top?
Society!

-157-

*H*ow do you know your girlfriend is too young for you?
When you have to make an airplane sound to put your dick in her mouth!

-158-

I've been in jail 5 minutes and already got raped

twice.

I'm fucking done playing monopoly with my dad!

-159-

A: My great grand-parents were in a concentration camp!
B: So was my grandpa. He died there!
A: I'm so sorry!
B: Poor fella fell out of the guard tower!

-160-

Son: Dad, is that guy about to die?
Dad: Judging by the size of that horse's cock I would say yes, son.

-161-

Son: Look daddy, I'm fixing the tire with a hammer!
Dad: Stfu!, you waste of sperm, kids your age are making iPhones in China.

-162-

A: Bro I have two bad news for you!
B: Combine them!
A: Your girlfriend is cheating on both of us!

-163-

They're going to start playing porn at the fuel pumps....
This is so you can watch someone else being fucked

at the same time as you.

-164-

Heard about the new shampoo for Pikeys?
It's called Go and Wash

-165-

Why do Japanese people have slanted eyes?
Because they're still squinting from the blast.

-166-

What's brown and runny?
Kelly Holmes.

-167-

I was watching the God channel with my disabled little sister the other day. After around thirty minutes, she rose from her wheelchair and walked across the room.
I stood up and screamed, "it's a miracle."
She turned round and replied, "no, I just can't stand to listen to this shit anymore," turned the TV off and collapsed in a heap in the middle of the room.

-168-

What is the difference between Jam and Jelly?
You can't jelly your dick up your girlfriend's arse!!

-169-

What's the difference between a lazy wife and the

England Football team?
Nothing- they both deserve to get beaten, and are lucky if they don't.

-170-

The other night I was invited out for a night with the 'girls.'
I told my husband that I would be home by midnight, 'I promise!' Well, the hours passed and the Blue Wkds went down way too easily.
Around 3 a.m., a bit pissed, I headed for home. Just as I got in the door, the cuckoo clock in the hallway started up and cuckooed 3 times. Quickly, realizing my husband would probably wake up, I cuckooed another 9 times.
I was really proud of myself for coming up with such a quick-witted solution, in order to escape a possible conflict with him. (Even when totally smashed... 3 cuckoos plus 9 cuckoos totals 12 cuckoos MIDNIGHT!)
The next morning my husband asked me what time I got in, I told him 'MIDNIGHT'... he didn't seem pissed off in the least.
Whew, I got away with that one! Then he said 'We need a new cuckoo clock.'
When I asked him why, he said, 'Well, last night our clock cuckooed three times, then said 'oh shit.'
Cuckooed 4 more times, cleared its throat, cuckooed another three times, giggled, cuckooed twice more, and then tripped over the coffee table and farted.

-171-

A teacher in class notices a little puddle below Suzie's chair.

"Ah, Suzie, why didn't you put your hand up?"

"I did, Miss, but it just ran through me fucking fingers."

-172-

A bloke is visiting his mother in a mental hospital when in the same room he comes across a guy moving his arms around and making beeping noises.

"Excuse me", he asks him. "What on earth are you doing?"

"I'm driving my car!, says the guy excitedly. "Beep, beep!"

"You fucking nut bar, you're not in a car, you're in a mental hospital!"

A voice comes from the bed opposite. "Mate, shut the fuck up will you, he's giving me twenty quid a day to wash the cunt."

-173-

How did Jesus really die??

He went into Somalia saying I am the bread of life.

-174-

In the indian last night when the waiter came over and said, "Curry ok sir", I said ok one song then Fuck off!

-175-

Only nowadays there appeared a possibility to realize yourself: sell your liver, kidney's, skeleton...

-176-

First thing this morning, there was a tap on my door. *Funny sense of humour my plumber has.*

-177-

The other day I needed to pay a visit to the public toilet, so I found a public toilet that had two cubicles. One of the doors was locked. So I went into the other one, closed the door, dropped my trousers and sat down.

A voice came from the cubicle next to me: "Hello mate, how are you doing? "

Although I thought that it was a bit strange, I didn't want to be rude, so I replied "Not too bad thanks. "

After a short pause, I heard the voice again "So, what are you up to? "

Again I answered, somewhat reluctantly, "Just having a quick shit... How about yourself? "

The next thing I heard him say was "sorry mate, I'll have to call you back. I've got some cunt in the cubicle next to me answering everything I say. "

-178-

How does every black joke begin? *With a look over your shoulder...*

-179-

I was walking in a cemetery this morning and seen a

bloke hiding behind a gravestone. I said "morning."
He replied, "No, just having a shit."

-180-

I can't think of anything worse, after a night of drinking, than waking up next to someone and not being able to remember their name, or how you met, or why they are dead.

-181-

I called that Rape Advice Line earlier today.
Unfortunately, it's only for victims.

-182-

Why don't black people go on cruises?
They're not falling for that one again.

-183-

I've just been to a Muslim birthday party.
The musical chairs was a bit slow but, fuck me, the pass the parcel was quick!

-184-

A family are driving behind a garbage truck when a dildo flies out and thumps against the windscreen. Embarrassed, and to spare her young sons' innocence, the mother turns around and says "Don't worry. That was an insect."
To which one of the boys replies "I'm surprised it could get off the ground with a cock like that."

-185-

How many Alzheimer's patients does it take to change a lightbulb?
To get to the other side.

-186-

Zebo, a half blind 5 year old African orphan has to ride 7 miles a day to school with only one leg on a bicycle with buckled wheels and no brakes.
Please give just a small donation of 2 pounds and we will send you the video it's fucking hilarious!!!

-187-

A dog is truly a man's best friend.
If you don't believe it, just try this experiment.
Lock your dog and your wife in the boot of the car for an hour.
When you open the boot, which one is really happy to see you?

-188-

I parked in a disabled space today and a traffic warden shouted to me...
"Oi, what's your disability?"
I said, "Tourette! now fuck off you cunt!"

-189-

A married man was having an affair with his

secretary.

One day, their passions overcame them and they took off for her house, where they made passionate love all afternoon. Exhausted from the wild sex, they fell asleep, awakening around eight PM. As the man threw on his clothes, he told the woman to take his shoes outside and rub them through the grass and dirt. Mystified, she nonetheless complied. He slipped into his shoes and drove home.

"Where have you been!" demanded his wife when he entered the house.

"Darling, I can't lie to you. I've been having an affair with my secretary and we've been having sex all afternoon. I fell asleep and didn't wake up until eight o'clock."

The wife glanced down at his shoes and said, "You lying bastard! You've been playing golf!"

-190-

A man came home from work, sat down in his favorite chair, turned on the TV, and said to his wife, "quick, bring me a beer before it starts."

She looked a little puzzled, but brought him a beer.

When he finished it, he said, "quick, bring me another beer. It's gonna start."

This time she looked a little angry, but brought him a beer.

When it was gone, he said, "quick, another beer, it's gonna start any second."

"That's it!" She blows her top. "You bastard! You waltz in here, flop your fat ass down, don't even say hello to me and then expect me to run around like

your slave. Don't you realize that I cook and clean and wash and iron all day long?"
The husband sighed. "Oh shit, it's started"

-191-

When I was a teenager, I used to pray every night that the girl next door would fancy me so that I could make love to her.
When I grew up, I realised that God didn't work like that, so I raped her and prayed for forgiveness.

-192-

If you have sex with a prostitute without her permission, is it rape... or shoplifting?

-193-

Why is the bible like a penis?
You get it forced down your throat by a priest.

-194-

We call our grandad "Spiderman".
He hasn't got any super powers - he just finds it difficult to get out of the bath.

-195-

British weather: it's just like a Muslim, either Sunni or Shi'ite.

-196-

Imagine my joy when I was getting out the Christmas decorations and found a present I forgot to give my kids last year. Their excited faces were a picture as they unwrapped it and opened the box.
Such a pity it was a puppy...

-197-

Women are like parking spaces, normally all the good ones are taken.
So, occasionally, when no one's looking, you have to stick it in a disabled one.

-198-

How do you know if you have a high sperm count?
When your wife has to chew before she swallows.

-199-

I wanked over a blind girl yesterday.
She never saw me coming.

-200-

Mummy takes little Johnny to the zoo. As they pass the elephant cage, the elephant has an erection.
"What's that, Mummy?" asks the child.
"Nothing, Johnny, nothing," says the embarrassed mother, swiftly leading him on.
A week later Johnny's dad takes him and the same happens. "What's that, Daddy?"
"That, son, is the elephant's penis."
"Mummy said it was nothing."

"Your mother's spoiled, Son!"

-201-

What's the difference between a gay and a microwave?

A microwave won't brown your sausage.

-202-

Little Johnny walks into his parents bedroom to find his Dad giving his Mum one. His Dad smirks and throws a pillow at the door saying, "Get out of here, you little shit!"

A couple of hours later Dad hears a whole lot of commotion coming from little Johnny's bedroom. He goes up to find little Johnny giving his Grandma a right royal seeing to.

Little Johnny smiles, "It's not so fucking funny when it's your Mum, is it?"

-203-

Did you hear about the look-a-like competition in China?

Everybody won.

-204-

Year 2 class in Bradford comes in from playtime.

Teacher asks Sarah: "What did you do at playtime?"

Sarah says, "I played in the sand box."

The teacher says, "That's good. Go to the blackboard, and if you can write 'sand' correctly, I'll give you a chocolate Hobnob."

She does and gets a chocolate Hobnob.

The teacher asks Michael what he did at playtime.

Michael says, "I played with Sarah in the sand box."

The teacher says, "Good. If you write 'box' correctly on the blackboard, I'll give you a chocolate Hobnob."

Michael does, and gets a chocolate Hobnob. Teacher then asks Mustaffa Abdulah Machimoudi what he did at playtime.

He says, "I tried to play with Sarah and Michael, but they threw rocks at me."

The teacher says, "Threw rocks at you? That sounds like blatant racial discrimination. If you can go to the blackboard and write 'blatant racial discrimination' I'll give you a chocolate Hobnob."

-205-

Apparently 60% of kids are overweight, and 72% of kids are having underage sex...

...so who is shagging all the fat kids?

-206-

Is that a gun in your pocket or are you just pleased to see me?

Bit of both, this is a rape.

-207-

A man returns home and find his wife with his best friend. He takes out the gun and shoots his friend to death. His wife:

- Listen, if you stay in such character, you will lose

all your friends.

-208-

I went to see the nurse this morning for my annual check-up.
She said I had to stop wanking.
When I asked why, she said, "because I'm trying to examine you!"

-209-

I was asked to run a marathon and I said, "no chance."
Then I was told it was for spastic and blind kids and I thought, "fuck it. I could win that!"

-210-

*T*wo sperms are having a race, one sperm says, "My arms are killing me with all this swimming, are we near the womb?"
The second sperm says, "Not for a long time yet, we've only just gone past her tonsils!!

-211-

*S*hannon Matthews mum burst into tears when she heard about the locked away Austrian Kids!!
She said later ...
All that fuckin wasted child benefit!

-212-

What does Elisabeth Fritzl have in her sandwiches?
Daddys Sauce.

-213-

Why doesn't Michael Barrymore have any ashtrays?
He puts his fags out in the pool.

-214-

A Taliban has been found dead at the bottom of Michael Barrymore's swimming pool.
Apparently it was a suicide bummer.

-215-

A Charity Pantomime in aid of Paranoid Schizophrenics and Homosexuals, descended into chaos yesterday when someone shouted "He's Behind You!".

-216-

Three friends -two straight guys and a gay guy -were on a cruise. A tidal wave came up and swamped the ship; they all drowned, and next thing you know, they're standing before St. Peter.
First came one of the straight guys and his wife. St. Peter shook his head sadly.
"I can't let you in. You loved money too much. You loved it so much, you even married a woman name Penny."
Then came the second straight guy.

"Sorry, can't let you in either. You loved food too much. You loved to eat so much, you even married a woman named Candy!"
The gay guy turned to his boyfriend and whispered nervously, "It doesn't look good, Dick."

-217-

Definition of a gay?
A bloke who enlarges the circle of his friends.

-218-

Five people have been found guilty of conspiracy to supply millions of pounds worth of counterfeit Viagra.
The judge described them as hardened criminals.

-219-

Two women were chatting.
"My 15 year old son is getting to be a right little bastard, hanging about in a gang, never coming to visit his grandparents with me - honestly, I sometimes think he wouldn't care if I died", the first woman said.
"I'm lucky in that respect", the second woman said, "My son is 22 now and loves his old mum, he snuggles up on the sofa with me of a night to watch TV, always gives me a kiss and hug whenever he is going out or going up to bed, we even do paintings together at weekends."
"I know", says the first woman "sometimes I wish my son had Down's Syndrome too."

-220-

What do Retards and Slinkys have in common?
Both are useless but give you a laugh when they fall down the stairs.

-221-

What's the difference between having a badly poured pint and having a child with Downs Syndrome?
If the head's too big on your beer you can blow it off.

-222-

A man is driving happily along in his car with his girlfriend when he's pulled over by the police.
The police officer approaches him and asks, "Have you been drinking Sir?"
"No. Why?" replies the man. "Was I all over the road?"
"No," replies the officer, "you were driving splendidly. It was the ugly fat bird in the passenger seat that made me suspicious."

-223-

A family of prostitutes are talking.
The daughter says, "I got £50 for a blow job today".
The mother says, "in my day it was £5".
The grandmother says, "In my day we were just glad for the warm drink".

-224-

If women are so perfect at multitasking,
How come they cannot have a Headache and Sex at
the same time ?

-225-

Womens personal ads guide (the real meanings):
- 40ish – 49;
- Adventurous - Slept with everyone;
- Athletic - No tits;
- Average looking – Ugly;
- Beautiful - Pathological liar;
- Contagious Smile - Does a lot of pills;
- Emotionally secure - On medication;
- Feminist – Fat;
- Free spirit – Junkie;
- Friendship first - Former very *friendly* person;
- Fun – Annoying;
- New Age - Body hair in the wrong places;
- Open-minded - Desperate Outgoing;
- Bitch -Sloppy drunk Professional;
- Voluptuous - Very Fat Large frame ;
- Stalker- Hugely Fat Wants Soul mate ;

-226-

My girlfriend told me last Christmas she wanted
something surprising and sexy.
Turned out she didn't mean rape.

-227-

Women don't want to hear men's opinions, they want to hear their own opinions but in a deeper voice.

-228-

What's the odd one out?

A: Washing Machine?
B: Toaster?
C: Woman?
D: Freezer?

B: Toaster - It's the only one that doesn't drip when it's fucked.

-229-

A woman is like a pack of Cards...
You need a Heart to love her,
You need a Diamond to win her,
You need a Club to smash her head in,
And a Spade to bury the bitch.

-230-

I like my whisky like my women. 15 years old and mixed with coke.

-231-

What is the first thing a battered wife does when she gets home from hospital?
The dishes and dinner if she's got any sense.

-232-

As an airplane is about to crash, a female passenger frantically jumps up, removes all her clothing and announces, "If I'm going to die, I want to die feeling like a woman. Is there anyone on this plane who is man enough?"
A man stands up, removes his shirt and says, "Here, iron this."

-233-

Bruce is driving over Harbor Bridge one day listening to some music in his car and just having a really great day. Suddenly he notices his girlfriend Sheila standing on the side of the bridge.
Bruce slams on the brakes, bolts out of the car and shouts, "Tanya! What the hell are you doing, babe?"
Tanya turns around with tears welling up in her eyes. "Bruce, honey! You got me pregnant. I don't want to be a burden, so I'm just gone to kill myself!"
Bruce gets a lump in his throat and climbs back into his car. "Tanya, not only are you a great fuck, but you're a good sport about it too!"

-234-

I bought a race horse and decided to call it "MY FACE".

Just imagine it running down the home straight with all the women shouting "COME ON MY FACE"!

-235-

Why is the part of a woman between her hips and her breasts called a waist?
Because they could have easily fitted in another pair of tits there.

-236-

Women's football!

-237-

A survey was recently conducted into why men enjoy blow jobs so much.
- 10% said they liked the physical feeling.
- 15% said they liked the dominance.
- 77% said they liked the 20 minutes of fucking silence.

-238-

Steve Jobs was an amazing man. He will live in my hard drive forever!

-239-

What has getting your girlfriend pregnant and locking your keys in the car got in common?
Both problems can be easily fixed with a coat hanger.

-240-

Police are investigating the bigger picture of Mark Speight's death.
It was sent in by 11 year old Susie from Reading.

-241-

Some mornings I wake up bitchy,
Other mornings I let her sleep.

-242-

What's the difference between Frenchmen and toast?
You can make soldiers out of toast.

-243-

What's long and hard and makes women groan?
An Ironing Board.

-244-

Two nuns, Sister Mary and Sister Elizabeth are walking through the park when they are jumped by two thugs. Their habits are ripped from them and the men begin to sexually assault them.
Sister Elizabeth casts her eyes heavenward and cries, "Forgive him Lord, for he knows not what he is doing!"
Sister Mary turns and moans, "Oh God, mine does!!!"

-245-

I used to hate weddings. All the old dears would

poke me and say: "You're next".
They soon stopped when I started saying the same to them at funerals...

-246-

A man says to his wife "Tell me something that will make me happy and sad at the same time."
His wife replies: "You've got a bigger dick than your brother"

-247-

What's the most sensitive part of your body when you're having a w*nk?
Your ears.

-248-

Murphy calls to see his mate Paddy, who has a broken leg.
Paddy says, "me feet are freezing mate, could you nip upstairs and get me slippers?"
"No bother," he says, and he runs upstairs and there are Paddy's two stunning 19 year old twin daughters sat on their beds.
"Hello dear girls, your Da' sent me up here to shag ya both."
"Fook off you liar!"
"I'll prove it," Murphy says.
So he shouts down the stairs, "both of them, Paddy?"
"Of course, what's the use of fookin' one?"

-249-

*E*ssex girl in bed with her boyfriend says, "How dare you call me a slapper?

"Get out of my bed right now, and you can take all your fucking mates with you too!"

-250-

A woman has been in a coma for 3 months, showing no signs of recovery.

One day, whilst giving her a bed bath, the nurse notices that there is a flicker on the monitor when they are cleaning her cunt.

The doctors send for her husband and tactfully explain the situation suggesting that he tries oral sex to see if it gets a bigger response.

So the medical staff draw the curtains to give him some privacy and await developments.

After about five minutes all the monitors suddenly go berserk and they rush in to find the woman stone dead.

"What happened?" demands a doctor...

"Dunno, reckon she mighta choked," comes the reply.

-251-

*M*e and the wife were trying roleplay in the bedroom last night.

She walked out in a huff after 30 seconds.

Apparently, asking your wife to pretend to be your daughter isn't very sexy.

✦ driver is pulled over by a policeman. The policeman approaches the drivers door.

"Is there a problem Officer?"

The policeman says, "Sir, you were speeding. Can I see your license please?"

The driver responds, "I'd give it to you but I don't have one."

"You don't have one? "

The man responds, "I lost it four times for drink driving. "

The policeman is shocked. "I see. Can I see your vehicle registration papers please? "

"I'm sorry, I can't do that. "

The policeman says, "Why not? "

"I stole this car. "

The officer says, "Stole it? "

The man says, "Yes, and I killed the owner. "

At this point the officer is getting irate. "You what? "

"She's in the boot if you want to see. "

The Officer looks at the man and slowly backs away to his car and calls for back up. Within minutes, five police cars show up, surrounding the car. A senior officer slowly approaches the car, clasping his half-drawn gun.

The senior officer says, "Sir, could you step out of your vehicle please! "

The man steps out of his vehicle. "Is there a problem sir? "

"One of my officers told me that you have stolen this car and murdered the owner. "

"Murdered the owner? "

The officer responds, "Yes, could you please open the boot of your car please? "

The man opens the boot, revealing nothing but an empty boot.

The officer says, "Is this your car sir? "

The man says "Yes" and hands over the registration papers.

The officer, understandably, is quite stunned. "One of my officers claims that you do not have a driving license. "

The man digs in his pocket revealing a wallet and hands it to the officer. The officer opens the wallet and examines the license. He looks quite puzzled.

"Thank you sir, one of my officers told me you didn't have a license, stole this car, and murdered the owner."

The man replies, "I bet you the lying bastard told you I was speeding, too! "

-253-

If you're bored and want to find out something amusing.

Go to internet movie database and in the search criteria type in the word wanker.

Quite fitting that this guy name comes up, the biggest wanker I can think of to be honest.

-254-

This morning on the way to work I drove into the back of a car, at some lights, whilst not really paying attention.

The driver got out... he was a dwarf.
He said, "I'm not happy"...
I replied, "Well, which one are you then?"

-255-

Me: Boss I am not coming into work to day coz I am sick.
Boss: How sick are you?
Me: Well I am in bed with my sister1

-256-

Q: How do you make a hormone?
A: Don't pay her.

-257-

Q: What did the poof do when he missed his boyfriend?
A: He shit in his hand and had a w*nk.

-258-

Q: Who is the most popular man in a nudist colony?
A: The guy who can carry two pitchers of beer and a foot of onion rings!

-259-

Q: Who is the most popular girl in a nudist colony?
A: The girl who can eat the last onion ring

-260-

Q: Why can't Jesus eat M&Ms?

A: They keep falling through the holes in his hands.

-261-

Q: What do you call a woman with no arms and no legs who gives good head?
A: Partially disabled.

-262-

If the Earth turned 30 times faster, we would get salary every day, but women would bleed to death...

-263-

Q: What's the similarity between a carton of milk and a woman?
A: They both need their flaps pushed back before you can get to the good bits.

-264-

Q: How do you know when your girlfriend is on anabolic steroids?
A: When she flips you over, holds you down and fucks you...up the arse with her clitoris.

-265-

A guy asks his waiter at a restaurant how they prepare their chicken.
The waiter goes blank for a second, then says, "Nothing special really... We just tell them they're going to die..."

-266-

-Mommy, Mommy! Are you sure this is the way to make ginger bread men?
-Shut up and get back in the oven.

-267-

In a hospital serving victims of land mines, a little girl wakes up from surgery.
Little Girl: Doctor, something is wrong... I can't feel my legs!
Doctor: Yes, we've had to amputate both your arms.

-268-

The McCartney kids are at the family ranch anxiously awaiting news of their mother. Paul emerges from his wife's bedroom "Kid's... there's good news and bad news."
"The bad news is your mother's strength and will to live has been sucked away by her awful disease and she died a few moments ago"
"The good news is.... It's steak and chips for dinner"

-269-

A leper walked into a bar and sat down. The bartender glanced over and promptly threw up all over himself and the floor.
The leper looked hurt and said, "Hey, I know I'm not exactly handsome, but I do have feelings and you could be a little sensitive about them."
The bartender, wiping his mouth on his sleeve, looked up and proclaimed, "I'm sorry as hell man, but it

wasn't you. That guy sitting next to you keeps dipping his scratchings in your neck."

-270-

Two men are sitting in a restaurant. There is also a gypsy woman sitting opposite to them with her legs wide spread.
One man says: "Look, she has such dark hair on her genitals!"
The other says: "Oh no, it isn't hair, it is dark panties!"
Then they made a bet - £100 . A waiter goes by so they ask him to find out for them.
He did so, but takes all the money and walks away.
"What happened, why are you taking the money?!" Asked the waiter.
He replies: "Neither of you was right! She had her period and there were flies on her!"

-271-

Two necrophiliacs are at work in the morgue. One of them turns to the other and says,
"You should have seen this woman they brought in last week. They pulled her out of the water after she'd been there for three weeks. Man, I'm tellin' you, her clit was just like a pickle."
"What," the other asks, "green?".
"No," says the first, " a bit sour."

-272-

Michael Jackson and his wife are in the recovery room with their new baby son.
The doctor walks in and Michael asks: "Doctor, how long before we can have sex?"
The doctor replies, "I'd wait until he's at least 14."

-273-

What's the worse thing about eating a bald cunt?
Putting the nappy back on afterwards

-274-

What's small brown and warm and found in the back of little boys underwear?
Michael Jacksons Hand!

-275-

After a particularly hard day at his trial MJs minder suggested that he has a quite night in to help calm him down ready for the next day.
"Why don't you get yourself a film Michael you like films".
"What a great idea!' says Michael " Can we get Aladin? "
"Aren't you in enough trouble?"

-276-

An SS guard at a concentration camp is inspecting a line of prisoners when he hears a sneeze
"Who sneezed?" he asks,

No one answers so he shoots five.
"Who sneezed?",
No answer, so he shoots five more.
"Who sneezed?",
Still no answer so five more are gunned down.
"Who sneezed?",
An old man puts his hand up.
"Come here" says the guard, the old man shuffles up.
"So, you sneezed eh?" The old guy nods,
"Bless you."

-277-

Man comes home from work to find his girlfriend by the door with her bags packed.
"I'm leaving you",
"Why? ",
"I've heard you're a peadophile",
"Bugger me",
"What? ",
"That's a big word for an eight year old".

-278-

What's worse than biting into an apple and finding a worm?
Being gang raped.

-279-

What goes 'BANG-BANG-BANG' (indicate with slapping motion on forhead)?
Paralympic Hurdeler.

What do you do after you've had sex with a 18 year old?
Wipe her blood off your cock onto her favourite teddy bear.

Two tramps are having a chat by the railway.
"I found this gorgeous girl tied to the tracks last week. Saved her before a train came, and then had 2 hours of the best sex of my life with her as a result",
"Really? Wow. Blonde or Brunette?"
"Don't know, couldn't find the head"

A tramp comes into a bar.
"Can I have a fork please?" He takes the fork and leaves. 2nd tramp walks in.
"Can I have a fork please?" He takes the fork and leave. 3rd tramp walks in.
"I guess you want a fork too?" says the barman,
"No, a straw please"
"How come you want a straw and the others wanted forks?"
"Someone been sick outside, and the others have already got the lumpy bits".

A spastic runs up to an ice cream man with his

career.

"Hello there, what can I do for you young man?",
asks the ice cream man

"Arrrrrsecreeeeem", replies the window licker,

"Certainly, what type would you like?",

"Garumph!",

"I'm sorry we don't have that flavor", he turns to the
career instead "What flavour would he like?"

"It doesn't matter", replies the career, "The little
spanner will only drop it".

-284-

"How was your day at school son?" enquires a caring
mum...

"I had sex with the math Teacher!"

"You did what? I'm ashamed of you, now go and tell
your Dad, what you have just told me!!!"

"Dad, I had sex with my math Teacher"

"Well done son, I'm proud of you, sit down and tell
me all about it"

"I cant, my arse hurts"!!

-285-

A young lad gets a magic set for Christmas but just
can't get one of the tricks right.

He asks his Dad for help, but his Dad says; "look son
I am a bit busy, go down the street and see the magic
bender" (the magic bender may/may not resemble
Paul Daniels).

The lad arrives at the magic bender's magic shop and
explains that he is having difficulty with his magic

tricks, the magic bender offers to help him out...

"Ok son", he says, bend over, take your pants down and tell me when you feel a finger up your arse...

The lad feels the finger squeezing up his ass and says "I feel it, I feel It".

The magic bender leans over his shoulder and says "Look no hands".

-286-

A man is getting ready to fuck his new girlfriend for the first time. He tries to push his dick in, but he can't get it in. He tries and tries, but to no avail. Finally he pushes inside her and starts giving it to her.

He says, "Damn, this hurts. It's so tight I can barely take it."

She says, "OK. Let me go to the bathroom and make it a little easier."

He climbs off and she disappears for a few moments. When she returns, she lays down and he climbs back on top of her. He slides in again, and this time it's much easier.

"Ahhh. That's more like it. Did you put some KY jelly in there?"

"Nope," she replies, "I just peeled off the fucking scabs..."

-287-

Two bums are walking along the side of a road early one morning, complaining about their empty stomachs. The night before they had spent every dime they had on whiskey, so naturally they had no money for breakfast. By and by they come upon a flattened possum lying dead on the roadside.

The first bum says to the second, "I'll split it with ya."

The second politely refuses, so the first bum eats the entire thing by himself. An hour or so later, as they are walking, the first bum starts turning green. He gags for a few minutes and then spews the possum remains all over the road.

The second bum smiles and says, "I knew if I waited long enough I'd get a hot meal."

-288-

Mary had her fill with the men she had had in her life and had just broken up with her latest beau. Determined to finally 'meet the One', she places an advert in the local paper's lonely hearts classified.

It said "Wanted - A man who will not hit me, not leave me but has to be an extremely wonderful lover."

Many weeks pass and not one answer to her ad... until there's a knock at the door. Mary goes to answer the door and opens it to see a man in a wheelchair with no arms or legs.

"I'm here about the ad" he says,

"How do I know you won't hit me?" says Mary.

"Well I have no arms so I cannot hit you even if I wanted to" he replied.

"How do I know you won't leave me?" says Mary.

"Well I have no legs so I cannot leave you even if I wanted to" he replied.

"How do I know that you're an extremely wonderful lover?" says Mary

"Well," begins the man, "what the fuck did you think I knocked the door with?".

-289-

Father's day, the most confusing day in the ghetto.

-290-

Olympic track makes you feel like you witnessed a crime, because you hear a gunshot and then see a bunch of black guys hauling ass.

-291-

A young girl with a bag is crossing the customs. Customs officers check her bag and find some kind of powder. They ask the girl:
- What kind of powder is that?
- Heroin
- But heroin is matte-white, and this powder is orange.
- This is a kids' heroine – orange taste.

-292-

One step forward, 12 floors down.

-293-

A ship with 30 sailors and one woman strands on a desert island. After one month the woman says:
- I can not proceed in this way.

And she suicides herself. After another month, the sailors say:
- We can not proceed in this way.
And they bury the woman. The next month, the sailors say:
- We can not proceed in this way.
And they dig up the woman.

-294-

My previous girlfriend had this weird sleeping disorder - in the middle of every night she would wake up and suck my dick.
No wonder her dad did not want her to move out.

-295-

I saw a man with one arm shopping in a second hand store.
I thought *"You are never going to find here what you are looking for"*...

-296-

Since it started to rain, my wife can't stop looking through the window.
If it will start pouring down, I'm afraid I will have to let her inside.

-297-

The judge asks the murderer:
- Why did you kill that old lady?
- For money..
- But you got only 20 cents

- Yes, but killing five of them would already make a dollar.

-298-

And these kids do not deserve a present from me, because they have not been eating well this year, - said Santa Claus, flying over the starving kids in Sudan.

-299-

It is genetically pre-recorded in men's brain to look for a women, which is alike his mother – said Mr. John to the judge at the court, where he was being blamed for raping his sister.

-300-

A Georgian man sits in the dock at the court, with his neck bended down. The judge:
- Why did you rape the girl?
- I liked her.
- Why did you raped the boy?
- I liked him
- Sir, why don't you look to my eyes when you talk to me?
- I'm afraid I'll like you…

ABOUT THE AUTHOR

Adam Smith is 28 years old, comedian from USA.
His mission is to make people smile until their belly hurts.
He has collected a vast collection of jokes and funny short stories that he wants to share with the entire   world!

Printed in Great Britain
by Amazon